Am I Naturally

4/99
AGD3378-1

Am I Naturally This Crazy?

Poems by Sara Holbrook

Boyds Mills Press

To my volleying partner,
Sharon Draper.
Many thanks
for your way with words.

Text copyright © 1996 by Sara Holbrook
Cover photograph copyright © 1996 by The Reuben Group

Published by Wordsong
Boyds Mills Press, Inc.
A Highlights Company
815 Church Street
Honesdale, Pennsylvania 18431
Printed in the United States of America

Publisher Cataloging-in-Publication Data
Holbrook, Sara.
    Am I naturally this crazy? / by Sara Holbrook.—1st ed.
[48]p. ; cm.
Summary : A collection of poems about feelings.
ISBN 1-56397-640-4
1. Feelings—Juvenile Poetry. 2. Children's Poetry, American.
[1. Feelings—Poetry. 2. American poetry.] I. Title.
811.54—dc20   1996   AC   CIP
Library of Congress Catalog Card Number 96-85173

First edition, 1996
Book designed by Tim Gillner
Cover concept and photography by The Reuben Group
The text of this book is set in 12-point Galliard.

10 9 8 7 6 5 4 3 2

TABLE OF CONTENTS

CONFUSED

Stacked and squashed.
Crammed and bruised.
My bureau looks a bit —
    confused.

A soccer shoe, a music box,
a china lamb,
five unmatched socks.
A magazine and candy wraps,
an old stuffed dog,
two baseball caps.
A Lego car, a floppy disk,
a watch, a comb,
one bowl (no fish).

Its drawers are drooling everywhere,
legs and sleeves and underwear.
Nearby a chair is nearly dressed
with cut-off jeans and Sunday best.

Above it all
a stickered mirror
reflects MY face.
I'm growing here!

BLUEPRINTS?

Will my ears grow long as Grandpa's?
What makes us look like kin?
Tell me where'd I get long eyelashes
and where'd I get my chin?

Where'd I get my ice cream sweet tooth
and this nose that wiggles when I talk?
Where'd I get my dizzy daydreams
and my foot-rolling, side-step walk?

Did I inherit my sense of humor
and these crooked, ugly toes?
What if I balloon like Uncle Harry
and have to shave my nose?

How long after I start growing
until I start to shrink?
Am I going to lose my teeth,
some day?
My hair?
My mind?

Do you think
I'll be tall or short or thin
or bursting at the seams?
Am I naturally this crazy?
Is it something in my genes?

I'm more than
who I am,
I'm also
who I'm from.
It's a scary speculation —
Who will I become?

NOT SO BAD

My best friend, Clean Jean,
makes her bed everyday.
Wears matched-up socks,
puts her dishes away.

She gets ribbons at swim meets
and *As* on her tests.
Her hair's always combed,
and her T-shirts look pressed.
Mom says I'm a good kid.
She means it, I guess.
But my room has exploded again.
What a mess.

My nightmares scare everyone
out of their sleep,
and I never find papers
that I'm s'posed to keep.

Did every kid once in a while
wet her pants?
Think about murder?
Eat in a trance?

Once, Jean's bike
was unlocked
and got swiped.
Boy, was her mother mad.
Could it be she's not perfect,
and I'm not so bad?

SELF-ESTEEM?

I tell my dog he's bad.
I laugh when he jumps and misses.
I gag when he drinks from the toilet
and then tries to give me kisses.
I mock how he twitches his nose,
and sometimes he makes me scream.
His nicknames are "Stinky" and "Hairball."

Can dogs get low self-esteem?

A NICE TRIP?

If I bumble-bump along,
klutz-awkward,
like some sloth-toed gangle-geek . . .

If I stupid-stumble slip
or free-fall flat
from foolish flappy feet . . .

If I trip
or just get stuck
knee-deep in quick-set doubt . . .

I know
I may look dumb.
But
do you have to point that out?

THROUGH THICK AND THIN

Of course.
I was wearing them yesterday.
And, yes.
I noticed the seams.
It's just
I like feeling comfortable.
These are my favoritest jeans.

I can't tell, you wouldn't believe,
all the scrapes that we've been in.
But I can tell you this,
they've stuck with me
through thick and thin.

We're always there for each other.
We run.
We leap.
We share the same feet.

We go to the mall
and we play ball
and then we fall
in bed to sleep.
I stand by them.
They stand by me,
even after I take them off.
If you washed them
people would think
these jeans and I
are getting soft!

THE BABYSITTER

The magnifying glass made the fire
on the dining room table.
I'm the one who put it out.
Good thing I'm fast with a bucket.
What's *she* upset about?

That babysitter's too sensitive.
I promise, it wasn't at all that bad.
In fact, I was pretty helpful.
I haven't a clue why she's mad.

Who'd have thought she'd twist like a tornado
over an itty bitty mouse.
It wasn't even loose.
It was safe there, in her blouse.

It was a joke!
I put the cat in the dryer,
but I only turned it to fluff.
Do I *smell* like cigars?
I swear, not even a single puff.

I know, I hid the channel selector,
but let's face it, she's a prude.
When my pop blew up in the freezer?
Guess what! I helped her wash the food.
I even cleaned up most of the glass
after I put my fist through the door.
And when we noticed the bloody footprints?
Why, I helped her wipe the floor.

When she cried, I brought her tissues,
but she only blubbered louder.
Don't you think she's overreacting?
Good grief.
You were only gone an hour.

OLD PICTURES

See that hole in my smile
and the pat on my head?
I was so old
I could make my own bed.

I could find my own boots
and zipper my coat,
pick up my toys
and tie my own bows.

I am much older
since I lost that tooth,
but you want to know
the honest-to-truth?

Grown-up gets scary,
and that is a fact.
If I had a brain
I'd have
put that tooth back.

WHO DID?

Stop! Halt!
My fault? My fault?
Your fault. Your fault.
Your fault. Your fault.
Who let anger in the house
to drop its bitter litter everywhere,
causing us to stumble,
grumble, slip and trip and glare?
You did. He did?
I did? She did.
You did. You did.
You did. You did.
It took over in a snap.
Who said anger was the boss?
Now we're up to here in grudges.
Someone tell it to get lost.
I should? I should?
He should. She should.
You should. You should.
You should. You should.
Oh, forget who let the anger in.
Blame games get so mean.
This mess is getting out of hand.
Let's all pitch in and clean.

BETTER THAN?

The snob
hides behind
a designer exterior
putting down others
and acting superior.

He's
the smoothest,
the richest,
most likely to win.
Which he'll tell you
before
you can even ask him.

He's
constantly buffing
his wax of perfection.
He shines
from a distance
but
not
on
closer
inspection.

GOOD STUFF

No one
  discounts who I am.
So listen up.
  I gotta tell you.
You can
  criticize away.
You won't degrade.
  I know my value.
Go ahead
  and take your little bites.
Your teeth
  will never touch my core.
You're acting
  so superior.
You can't digest
  that I'm worth more.
Stuck ups
  are bad company.
You think
  that I'm not good enough?
Just because
  I'm not perfection
doesn't mean
  I'm not good stuff.

NEEDY CAT

She nuzzles up,
head begging
for a loving pat,
then turns away,
soft purring,
without looking back.
Pretending independence,
that needy little cat.

A love
is what she wants.
Aloof
is what you see.
I'd probably ignore her
if she weren't
a lot like me.

SOME FAMILIES

Some families are extended
with grandmothers and aunts,
with cousins by the dozens.
No one has a chance
to say which ones they choose
and which they want removed.
Then, family's what they got,
a little or a lot.
Some families start small
counting fingers while they grow,
others simply shrink, or take off for the coast.
Some families divide
and then get rearranged.
When grown-ups choose new partners
the family dance gets strange.
Some people think the family thing
is mostly overrated.
Some people feel left out,
and some stay isolated.
Some people pick each other
and who knows who's behind it;
they bunch up like bouquets,
and family's where they find it.

LABELS

People wear labels,
like African American,
Native American,
White,
Asian, Hispanic or
Euro-Caucasian —
I just ask that you get my name right.
I'm part Willie,
part Ethel,
part Suzi and Scott.
Part assembly-line worker,
part barber, a lot of dancer
and salesman. Part grocer and mailman.
Part rural, part city, part cook
and part caveman.
I'm a chunk-style vegetable soup
of cultural little bits,
my recipe's unique
and no one label fits.
Grouping folks together
is an individual waste.
You can't know me by just a look,
you have to take a taste.

VALENTINE

I gave Jim a valentine.
He stuffed it in his shirt,
then stood there in the hallway
with his jerko friends and smirked.

I must be dumber than a doorknob,
but I thought I'd take a chance.
Now, my foot is itching in my shoe,
it wants to kick his pants.

My hands are searching
for a hiding place.
They want to choke his throat.
He thinks that I'm a joke.

One day I hope he feels
what burned is all about,
and he will learn too late
that love's too fine to be crumped out.

BEFORE YOU START TO HEAL

You have to listen to divorce,
because you know it's real.
Of course
it beats you up inside,
and sometimes you must hide
just how bad you feel.
And sometimes you must cry,
stomp and wonder why.
Wish that it weren't so.
Wish that it weren't so.

Divorce is louder than a shout,
and you can't call "time out."
And sometimes
out of fear,
divorce is hard to hear.
But, still you have to feel,
recognize what's real.
Before you start to heal.
Before you start to heal.

SUBTLE

Subtle
isn't a punch in the nose,
a kick in the shins,
a bee in the toes.

Subtle
stays quiet,
yet
everyone knows.

WANTED?

I never wanted step parents,
  step sisters or step dogs.
In fact, I like the thought about
  as much as kissing frogs.

I never wanted holidays
  to come "Home" and "Away,"
with halftime in the car
  so both teams get to play.

I never wanted to sit and add up
  all the "normal" things I've missed.
Don't ask me WHAT I wanted,
  I just never wanted this.

SORRY

Sorry
follows like my shadow,
fastened at the heels.
It trails me to my room
and sits with me at meals.

It nags me in my dreams
when I have gone to bed.
That Sorry pest hangs on
until it's finally said.

WHAT'S FAIR?

It's not fair.
I have to share
my games, my bike, my sweater.
It's not right
that parents fight.
Isn't there a better
way to stay
than in this family way?

It's tempting just to hate
the word
"cooperate"
when you're arguing who's boss.
It's too bad
the times we had
to listen through tight jaws.

Some of my maddest times
I think
alone's the way to live.
And other times I'm glad
I have
a family to forgive.

CAN'T WAIT

I can't wait.
I can't wait.
This waiting's a strain.
My excitement's so loud
it scribbled my brain.
Hurry and hurry,
this waiting's a pain.
Pushing and jumping,
tap, tap, pant and pace.
I wish I could broad jump
outta this place.

I wish I could vanish.
I wish I could fly.
You told me to wait,
but you didn't say why
or how much or how long.
Let's go and get going.
Let's don't hang around.
Your slow-motion motions
are groaning me down.

HOME ALONE

I'm just sitting here . . . thinking —
of monsters and ghosts
and which spooky movies
I hate the most.
I remember that robbery
I heard of last week
where they chopped up some guy
and stole both his feet.

You can tell me,
  "Don't think that,
  you'll only get stressed."
But my head spins around,
it's like I'm possessed.
There's that face in the window,
that creak on the stairs.
Those snakes in the toilet.

Those rats — over there.
Sure, I know that this scared stuff
is all in my mind.
Still.
I sit so I can't get attacked from behind
with a blood-coated knife or a gun or a wire.
Then?
If I start to get bored, I just smell up a fire,
and think —
What would I save?
Who would survive?
How would it feel
to be barbecued live?
I imagine my pain
and practice a groan.

What do you do
when you're home alone?

FEELINGS MAKE ME REAL

You are not the boss of me
and what I feel inside.
Please don't say,
"Let's see a smile,"
or tell me not to cry.

I am not too sensitive.
You think my inside's steel?
You can't tell me how to be,
feelings make me real.

SLIPPED

I slipped.
Everything seems to stink.
I better
check my shoe.
I can't tell
where or when
but, yes,
I guess,
I stepped in a rotten mood.
Peeeee-u!

NEVER TRUST A MOTHER

My mother has these sunglasses,
they make her look like a bug.
And
she never waits till we're alone
to slap on a kiss and a hug.

She has this special voice
when she pipes up on my behalf.
She wears the dumbest shoes
IN PUBLIC.
And
have you heard my mother laugh?

You think your mother's bad?
Just imagine,
my mother SINGS!
She's usually impossible to control
but I've learned a couple important things.

Never trust a mother with embarrassing stories,
naked pictures in the bathtub,
or childish habits involving hands.
Mothers just can't help themselves—
they blurt them out like marching bands.

And
all mothers are more than just the smile and the
handshake,
which is all the average person sees.
'Cause when it comes to embarrassing their kids . . .
all mothers have advanced degrees.

LOSING MY SENSES

My smeller is stopped,
it hurts when I speak.
I'm cold in the toes
and hot in the cheek.

I couldn't taste chili peppers,
I am plugged but I drain.
My ears are all jammed
and my head's a big pain.

I'm losing my senses
one by one
ever since my poor nose
went red-on-the-run.

IT'S ME, GOING PLACES

Day meets Darkness,
corner of Dusk and Dawn.
They scratch and they yawn
with familiar faces
before shaking hands
and trading places.

I'm asleep until the alarm
pistol starts
my washing and brushing,
running laps of
bedroom to bathroom to bedroom,
strip, dress and flushing.
No time to sigh
as a tired mirror faces
my sleepy-eyed
fumbling with
buttons and laces.
Days aren't born busy,
it's me, going places.
Day arrives calm.
Me?
I'm off to the races.

WHAT'S REAL?

Pictured between reruns
and what commercials want to sell,
explodes another war
in some far place
that I can't spell.

To me,
war appears as broken bodies,
burning buildings,
and smoking gas,
interrupted by auto salesmen,
frosty colas,
and kitchen wax.

Every evening
around dinner
devastation
is served up with my meal,
then sprinkled with laundry powder.
It's hard to tell.

Which pictures are real?

CAN WE BE FRIENDS?

I have had an overview
of little bits
of all of you.
I circle for a place to land.
Trying to find the best approach,
looking casual,
unplanned.

I'm not up for showing off
and I don't want to pretend.
No high-flying acrobatics —
I just want to be your friend.

JUST IMAGINE

Loves me . . .
Loves me not . . .
Loves me . . .
Loves me not . . .

The petal-popping,
forehead-bopping,
heartbeat-stopping
question.
Leaves me
sometimes singing,
then eyeballs stinging,
both hands wringing
crazy.

Is it love?
How can I know?
Just imagine
if it were so.

I'd be calm,
since I would know,
Love,
not craziness
would grow.

Just imagine
if it were so.
Just imagine
if it were so.

Just imagine if it were so!

Ah . . .

RACING WITH RISK

I stopped to ask a
squirrel
about a fact
that's little known,
a silent eyeball chat.
No one was looking,
we were alone.
Branched out in that tree,
sniffing at the breeze,
he let me come this close
and count his whiskers and his toes.

I asked, "Squirrels climb and chase
all 'round the place,
bossing as they go.
But some squirrels at play
get blown away.
Why *do* squirrels cross the road?"

He was ready to race with risk,
a little bit like me,
but small, his hands locked in
a starting block of tree.

"What are you, crazy?
Curious?
Bored?"
I asked, "Are you nut-starved
or just lost your senses?
Wouldn't you be better off
protected behind tall fences?
That way you'd be safe . . . "

He stared his black beads
straight at me.
Winked.
And off he raced.

PART OF THE JOB DESCRIPTION

Nature
gives us a mother
to fry our chicken,
shrink our sweatshirts
and spoil our fun.
But like pillows,
it's a pain in the neck
to have to juggle
more than one.
It's her job
to ask me to explain
where I was
and what I did.
It's not your job,
it's hers,
to make me feel
like a little kid.

ORDINARY

What if I'm never rich
or a princess,
or a king?
What if I never am an astronaut
or quarterback a team.
I love to dream.

But if I never am a rock star
or don't grow up Ivy League;
if I never go to state
or read my name on a marquee;
If I don't have my say on talk shows
or have cards marked "CEO;"
thank my mom in front of
thousands,
play Olympic,
bring home gold;
what dreams will picture
when I sleep?
What is the label that I'll carry?

How will I know if I succeed?
Where is the fame in ordinary?

COMING SOON

I am how I act
and
I am what I eat.
I sometimes react
and
I'm not yet complete.

Nothing about me is permanent.
Growing up
is a chain reaction.
The mirror may reflect
  "ugly duckling,"
but inside I'm a
  "coming attraction."